A FRIEND IN THE LIBRARY

HISTORY AND BIOGRAPHY I

BY

EVA MARCH TAPPAN

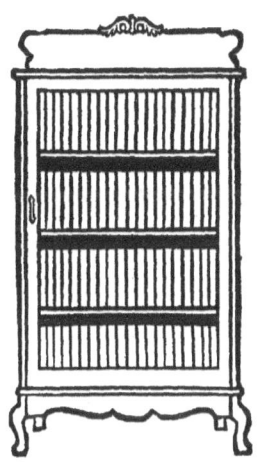

British Library Cataloguing-in-Publication Data
A catalogue record for this book is available from the
British Library

HISTORY AND BIOGRAPHY, I

A FRIEND IN THE LIBRARY

A Practical Guide to the Writings of

RALPH WALDO EMERSON

NATHANIEL HAWTHORNE

HENRY WADSWORTH LONGFELLOW

JAMES RUSSELL LOWELL

JOHN GREENLEAF WHITTIER

OLIVER WENDELL HOLMES

IN TWELVE VOLUMES

VOLUME IV

Eva March Tappan

Eva March Tappan was born on 26th December 1854 in Blackstone, Massachusetts, America. She is well known as a factual as well as fictional writer, but spent her early career as a teacher. Tappan was the only child of Reverend Edmund March Tappan and Lucretia Logée, and received her education at the esteemed Vassar College. This was a private coeducational liberal arts college, in the town of Poughkeepsie, New York, from which she graduated in 1875. Here, Tappan was a member of Phi Beta Kappa, the oldest honour society for the liberal arts and sciences, widely considered as the nations most prestigious society. She also edited the *Vassar Miscellany,* a college publication.

After leaving her early education, Tappan began teaching at Wheaton College, one of the oldest institutions of higher education for women in the United States, founded in 1834 and based in Norton, Massachusetts. She taught Latin and German here, from 1875 until 1880, before moving on to the Raymond Academy in Camden, New Jersey where she was associate Principal until 1894. Tappan also received a graduate degree in English Literature from the University of Pennsylvania. This allowed her to pursue her first love, that of reading and writing, and she taught as head of the English department at the English High School at Worcester, Massachusetts.

It was only after this date that Tappan began her literary career, writing about famous characters in history, often aimed at educating children in important historical themes and epochs. Some of her better known works include, *In the Days of William the Conqueror* (1901) and *In the Days of Queen Elizabeth* (1902), *The Out-of-Door Book* (1907), *When Knights Were Bold* (1911) and *The Little Book of the Flag* (1917). Tappan never married, being a happy singleton, and died on 29th January 1930, aged seventy-five.

HISTORY AND BIOGRAPHY, I

IT occurred to me one day that it would be worth while to see to what extent American history and biography had been related by our six poets. The more I read, the more interesting the search became, for I found it quite possible to follow along in their poems and sketches the main events of our history and the lives of a large number of our leading men.

The colonial period is especially rich in legends and traditions, in bits of real history, and bits of history half hidden by a golden mist of poetry and romance. Looking back to the days before the coming of Columbus, we find Longfellow's "Skeleton in Armor" (i. 63). The poet had seen a skeleton with a breastplate of brass, which had been dug up at Fall River. Many people thought these were the remains of some hardy Norseman who had made his way to our shores eight or nine hundred years before. The idea occurred to Longfellow of connecting this with the Round Tower at Newport, the "Old Stone Mill," and therefore he wrote of the viking bold who had stolen a

> Blue-eyed maid,
> Yielding, yet half afraid,

his prince's daughter, and, beating through the hurricane, had brought her to the New World.

> There for my lady's bower
> Built I the lofty tower,
> Which, to this very hour,
> Stands looking seaward.

If one wishes to follow still further back into the viking life, he will find the "Musician's Tale" in Longfellow's "Tales of a Wayside

Inn" (iv. 56), a collection of stories of Thor, King Olaf, Thora, Sigrid, and other characters of mythology or legend.

Longfellow was a man of the highest culture; but he had a warm liking for the beginnings of things, the simple ways of the colonists, and the life of the Indians; and he planned to weave together the beautiful Indian traditions into one poem. This was the origin of "Hiawatha" (ii. 123), the story of the child who

> Learned of every bird its language,
> Learned their names and all their secrets;

the young brave who

> Could shoot ten arrows upward,
> Shoot them with such strength and swiftness,
> That the tenth had left the bow-string
> Ere the first to earth had fallen!

the lover of

> Minnehaha, Laughing Water,
> Loveliest of Dacotah women!

Hiawatha becomes the leader and teacher and protector of his people; but at last the time comes when he knows that he must bid them farewell and go

> On a long and distant journey,
> To the portals of the Sunset,
> To the regions of the home-wind.

Then the people and the forests and the waves and the birds say farewell to him whom they love, and he departs

> To the Islands of the Blessed,
> To the kingdom of Ponemah,
> To the land of the Hereafter!

Longfellow's "Courtship of Miles Standish" (ii. 301) belongs of course to the early days of Massachusetts. So does Whittier's "The Swan Song of Parson Avery" (i. 188), the story of the good man who "with his wife and children eight" was wrecked "on the Rock of Avery's Fall."

These Pilgrims and Puritans were great lovers of education, and glad enough they were when one Master Ezekiel Cheever crossed the seas and came to teach the small boys in one colony after another. Hawthorne has written an account ("The Old-Fashioned School," xii. 96) of the "queer looking little fellows, wearing square-skirted coats and small clothes, with buttons at the knee," who became his pupils and trembled before the stern Master with his birchen rod; but no one must laugh at them, for they were afterwards some of the great folk of Boston. The school-houses were, as Lowell called them ("New England Two Centuries Ago," iv. 3), "An original kind of fortification invented by the founders of New England. They are," he says, "the martello-towers that protect our coast . . . the first row of trammels and pothooks which the little Shearjashubs and Elkanahs blotted and blubbered across their copy-books, was the preamble to the Declaration of Independence." The town school would fit the ordinary "little Shearjashubs and Elkanahs" for life; but he who was to become the great man of the colony, the grave and reverend minister, must, like the bee that is to become a queen, be fed upon food of even greater excellence. He must go to college and learn to read Greek and Hebrew and Chaldee and "Syriack." Harvard was founded;

And who was on the Catalogue
When college was begun?

Two nephews of the President,
And *the* Professor's son.
(They turned a little Indian by,
As brown as any bun;)
Lord! how the seniors knocked about
The freshman class of one! [1]

That "Indian question" was a puzzle. The
French taught the "Salvages" Christianity,
but treated them, whether Christian or heathen,
with an easy-going comradeship that won their
liking. In the more serious life of New England, Indians must either become Christians,
after the school of the Puritans, or else they
were regarded as a species of evil spirit, to be
exterminated as enemies of the Lord. But John
Eliot, minister of Roxbury, looked upon them
just as he would have looked upon white men

[1] "A Song for the Centennial Celebration of Harvard College," 1836, Holmes, xii. 73.

who needed teaching. He learned their language and translated the Bible for them. He opened schools and taught them to read and to pray. Hawthorne has told the story of his work for them in one of his children's books (xii. 46), and Whittier has written about one of the "praying Indians" in his "Nauhaught, the Deacon" (i. 304). If all the colonists and discoverers could have been John Eliots, the many stories of Indian massacres might never have been written. Whittier narrates ("The Boy Captives," vi. 395) the capture of two boys who finally managed to make their escape from the Indians; but in the same sketch he says that an ancestor of his own, true to his Quaker principles, refused to go to the neighboring fort for refuge or even to take up arms to defend his life and prop-

8

erty. He treated the red men kindly, and in their wildest raids they left him unharmed.

The troubles of the colonists were many, and among the most perplexing of them was the coming of the Quakers. Home and friends and comfort had been given up for the desolate shores of a new country, that these early settlers might worship God as they thought right and bring up their children in the way they believed that children should go. Behold, the Quakers came upon them, firmly convinced in their consciences that it was their duty to preach to these benighted colonists and convert them from the error of their ways. The irresistible force had met the immovable body, and it is no wonder that there was trouble. With blackened face, ashes on her head, and a bit of sackcloth wound about her, a

Quaker woman walked into the "Old South" in time of service and bade the worshipers repent. In these days she would have been soothed and gently led away for quiet and medical treatment, but in those times insanity was regarded as the work of Satan, and the insane were chained and starved and cruelly beaten, in the hope of exorcising the evil spirit that had possessed them. What wonder that, as Whittier describes the scene ("The Old South," i. 371), she was whipped at the cart-tail in the streets of the town? His "How the Women Went from Dover" (i. 400) is another tale of the punishment of the Quakers, and of the brave Justice Pike of Salisbury. He read the warrant: —

> *"These convey*
> *From our precincts; at every town on the way*

Give each ten lashes." "God judge the brute!
I tread his order under my foot!

"Cut loose these poor ones and let them go;
Come what will of it, all men shall know
No warrant is good, though backed by the Crown,
For whipping women in Salisbury town!"

Whittier thoroughly enjoys telling the tale
when, as sometimes happened, the Quakers
got the better of it. His "The King's Missive"
(i. 381) tells how

Under the great hill sloping bare
    To cove and meadow and Common lot,
In his council chamber and oaken chair,
    Sat the worshipful Governor Endicott,
A grave, strong man, who knew no peer
In the pilgrim land, where he ruled in fear
Of God, not man, and for good or ill
Held his trust with an iron will.

The clerk enters and whispers that

A FRIEND IN THE LIBRARY

A fellow banished on pain of death —
Shattuck of Salem, unhealed of the whip,

has dared to return. Then

Into that presence grim and dread
Came Samuel Shattuck, with hat on head.

"Off with the knave's hat!" An angry hand
    Smote down the offence; but the wearer said,
With a quiet smile, "By the King's command
    I bear his message and stand in his stead."
In the Governor's hand a missive he laid
With the royal arms on its seal displayed,
And the proud man spoke as he gazed thereat,
Uncovering, "Give Mr. Shattuck his hat."

The Quaker messenger might well look at the
stern governor "with a quiet smile," for the
letter commanded that the Quakers in prison
should be set free. Longfellow in his "John
Endicott" (v. 355) has written a tragedy on
the same subject.

Another matter which harassed the brains and hearts and consciences of the poor colonists was the question of witchcraft. Quakers they could punish — if the king would permit; and could drive away —if they could only be kept away; and, however troublesome they might be, they were at least men and women, and nothing save their heretical influence need be feared. Witchcraft was immeasurably worse, for now the struggle was against invisible foes, against evil spirits and demons who made their lurking-places in the vast and unexplored wilderness. Strange voices had been heard in the forest, the people of Newbury had seen a double-headed snake, and the people of New Haven had seen a ship in the air. This vision of the ship, however, they firmly believed was sent them in answer to their prayers that they might know the fate of their friends at sea. Longfellow has made the story into rhyme ("The Phantom Ship," iii. 19), and has told it in almost the very words of Cotton Mather, minister of the North Church in Boston. Mather was a learned man. He could write in seven languages, he owned the largest library in the colonies, and he had read it through and through. He believed in witchcraft; and, indeed, how could he help it? The wonder is not that any one believed in witches, but rather that any one ventured to doubt their existence. Hundreds of thousands of so-called witches had been put to death in Europe. Within the memory of elderly men among the colonists, more than one hundred and fifty people in two of the English counties had been tried for witchcraft and pronounced guilty. The English laws against it were binding at the time of the "Salem witchcraft," and endured for many years later. It would have been a marvel indeed if the colonists had cut loose from all the beliefs of their friends "at home." Longfellow in his "Giles Corey" (v. 445) brings before us a vivid picture of the

Delusions of the days that once have been,
Witchcraft and wonders of the world unseen,
Phantoms of air, and necromantic arts,
That crushed the weak and awed the stoutest hearts.

The warfare with the Indians was not quieted, but broke out from time to time. One encounter, that of Lovell's, or Lovewell's, Pond, gave Longfellow, then a boy of thirteen, a subject for his first poem that appeared in print ("The Battle of Lovell's

Pond," i. 327). His verses were published by a Portland paper. There is no special mark of genius about them; and yet they are very different from the doggerel of a "long and mournful ballad" that some one wrote on the same subject, which says,

> What time the noble Lovewell came
> With fifty men from Dunstable,
> The cruel Pequot tribe to tame
> With arms and bloodshed terrible.

In the midst of the colonial troubles, it is refreshing to come upon one man who knew just what he wanted and succeeded in getting it, — the carpenter lad who set his heart upon having a "fair brick house" on Green Lane in Boston. A few years passed and his wish came true. He had not only a "fair brick house," but great bags of silver dollars, cups of gold, and even a table of solid silver. Hawthorne has told the wonder-tale of how this came about; indeed, he has told it twice, once for children ("The Sunken Treasure" xii. 69) and once for grown folk ("Sir William Phips," xvii. 13). But the version for children is the more interesting and has quite as much information.

There is another story of events that came to pass a few years later, the account of an expedition in which New England, New York, and New Jersey knew what they wanted and contrived to get it, even though it was to capture Louisburg, the strongest fortress in America. The plan had "a lawyer for contriver, a merchant for general, and farmers, fishermen, and mechanics for soldiers" — and they took the fort! It is no wonder that

Hawthorne wrote two accounts of such a feat as that ("The Provincial Muster," xii. 132; and "Sir William Pepperell," xvii. 23).

Ten years after the capture of Louisburg the "French Neutrals" of Acadia, or Nova Scotia, were accused by the English of aiding the French against their English rulers. Their homes were destroyed and they were carried away and distributed among the British colonies of the coast. It was a cruel deed; but war is always cruel. A little while before this the king of France had hoped to capture New York, and if he had succeeded, he had meant to do this same thing to the people of the English colony. Hawthorne wrote a short account of the destruction of the Acadian villages in his "Grandfather's Chair" ("The Acadian Exiles," xii. 147). A few years later, he heard the story that among the unhappy exiles were a young couple who on their marriage day were separated by the officers. All her life long the bride wandered through the colonies, searching for her bridegroom. In her old age she found him — on his death-bed. One would think this was just the plot that would appeal to Hawthorne, but for some reason it did not. "If you really do not want this incident for a tale," said Longfellow, "let me have it for a poem." So it was that "Evangeline" (ii. 3) was begun. Much of it was written with a pencil, in a darkened room, to spare the author's eyes; and when it was completed, he wrote in his journal, "When evening came, I really missed the poem and the pencil." Hawthorne was delighted with "Evangeline." Whittier called it "a psalm of love and for-

giveness." Holmes declared that of all Longfellow's longer poems this was the masterpiece. It is as smooth and graceful and beautiful as a poem can be; but under all the
beauty and grace lies a foundation of strength
and firmness, the power of love in the con-
stant heart of a faithful woman.

In the days between the expulsion of the
Acadians and the Revolutionary War, a man
named John Woolman went wandering up
and down the land, journeying hither and
thither, wherever he believed himself led by
the hand of God, that he might do the work
of God. He was a Friend, and he went from
home to home of the people of his sect. In his
early life he had made up his mind that slavery
was wrong, and it was a question with him
how to accept the ever-ready hospitality of the

Friends who were slaveholders. At length he settled it by insisting upon giving to his hosts money to pay for his entertainment. This was contrary to the custom of Friends and was not an agreeable thing for a shy, sensitive man to do; and it was not pleasant for the generous-hearted, guest-loving planters; but after a little talk with him, they could not help seeing his sincerity, and, as he said, the way was made easier than he expected. He kept a journal, and Whittier wrote for its publication an appreciative, sympathetic introduction, which is of much interest by itself and well worthy to stand alone (" John Woolman's Journal," vii. 315).

Coming nearer to the times of the Revolution, any one could guess that Holmes would never pass by so tempting a subject for verse

as the Boston Tea-Party. He wrote his poem
("A Ballad of the Boston Tea-Party," xiii.
57) for a meeting of the Massachusetts Historical Society, but it has not quite so much of
seriousness as one might expect of a paper
prepared for so dignified an assemblage. He
says : —

> No! ne'er was mingled such a draught
>   In palace, hall, or arbor,
> As freemen brewed and tyrants quaffed
>   That night in Boston Harbor!
> It kept King George so long awake
>   His brain at last got addled.
> It made the nerves of Britain shake
>   With seven-score millions saddled.
>
>   .   .   .   .
>
> Fast spread the tempest's darkening pall,
>   The mighty realms were troubled;
> The storm broke loose, but first of all
>   The Boston teapot bubbled!

From the bubbling of the "Boston teapot" to the first guns of the Revolution was but two years. Longfcllow tells the story of the night before the battles of Lexington and Concord in his "Paul Revere's Ride," the first of the "Tales of a Wayside Inn" (iv.). The "Land-lord" is the narrator, and Longfellow pictures him as

> A man of ancient pedigree,
> A Justice of the Peace was he,
> Known in all Sudbury as "The Squire."
> Proud was he of his name and race,
> Of old Sir William and Sir Hugh,
> And in the parlor, full in view,
> His coat-of-arms, well framed and glazed,
> Upon the wall in colors blazed;
>
> .   .   .   .
>
> And over this, no longer bright,
> Though glimmering with a latent light,

A FRIEND IN THE LIBRARY

> Was hung the sword his grandsire bore
> In the rebellious days of yore,
> Down there at Concord in the fight.

No one could have done fuller justice to the story of the warning of the Middlesex farmers than Longfellow. The whole poem is most excellent, but there is one line in particular that is wonderfully fine, —

> The fate of a nation was riding that night,

because it expresses so much in so few and so simple words. The ability to say much in little is a sure sign of strength. Longfellow's poems ripple along smoothly and pleasantly, but when strength is needed he never fails us.

On the morning after Paul Revere's ride,

> Slowly the mist o'er the meadow was creeping,
> Bright on the dewy buds glistened the sun,
> When from his couch, while his children were sleeping,
> Rose the bold rebel and shouldered his gun.

Waving her golden veil
Over the silent dale,
Blithe looked the morning on cottage and spire;
Hushed was his parting sigh,
While from his noble eye
Flashed the last sparkle of liberty's fire.

So it is that Holmes begins his poem on the first day of the Revolution ("Lexington," xii. 67). His verse is earnest and patriotic, but the metre is rather too jaunty for a battle-poem. Scott uses this metre for his "Boat Song" in the "Lady of the Lake":—

Hail to the chief who in triumph advances!

but it is not serious enough to tell the tale of so defiant a resistance, so stern a defense of home and principle as the warfare of that famous day. The metre of Whittier's "Lexington" (iv. 201) is far more dignified.

Their feet had trodden peaceful ways;
  They loved not strife, they dreaded pain;
  They saw not, what to us is plain,
That God would make man's wrath his praise.

Lowell, too, wrote a poem on that first day of the Revolution, his "Ode Read at the One Hundredth Anniversary of the Fight at Concord Bridge" (xiii. 73). Some of the lines in this are exceedingly fine; for instance: —

Here English law and English thought
'Gainst the self-will of England fought;
And here were men (coequal with their fate),
Who did great things, unconscious they were great.

We are inclined to think of the Revolutionary heroes as merely embodiments of patriotism, standing on Bunker Hill and firing at "the whites of their eyes," or signing the Declaration of Independence; and it is good to find Lowell remembering that they were people like us, who loved their homes and their families. In this same ode he says :—

Think you these felt no charms
In their gray homesteads and embowered farms?
In household faces waiting at the door
Their evening step should lighten up no more?
In fields their boyish feet had known?
In trees their fathers' hands had set,
And which with them had grown,
Widening each year their leafy coronet?
Felt they no pang of passionate regret
For those unsolid goods that seem so much our own?
These things are dear to every man that lives,
And life prized more for what it lends than gives.

At the end of this division of the poem is the noble thought, —

Men come to learn in grateful pilgrimage,
That length of days is knowing when to die.

Lowell wrote a shorter poem on the same

subject, "Lines Suggested by the Graves of Two English Soldiers on Concord Battle-Ground" (ix. 271). Particularly good is his

> Two graves are here: to mark the place,
> At head and foot, an unhewn stone,
> O'er which the herald lichens trace
> The blazon of oblivion.

His never-failing sympathy reveals itself in the lines,

> Unheard, beyond the ocean tide,
> Their English mother made her moan.

The story of the second day after the battle of Lexington has been told by the pen of Whittier. "The 21st of April, 1775," he says, "witnessed an awful commotion in the little village of Ipswich." The British "regulars" were coming, so said rumor, arising from no one knows where. The able-bodied men had marched to Cambridge and Lexington. There was nothing to do but flee. In the wild frenzy, silver was thrown into the wells, the cat was carried away to safety, and the baby was left behind; and it seemed as if most of the people had left their reason behind with the baby. In "The Great Ipswich Fright" (vi. 380), Whittier tells the ending of the tale, which is much like that of the old nursery rhyme, —

The King of France and twenty thousand men
Marched up the hill and then marched down again;

for the British were not coming at all; but the fright was very severe while it lasted.

Holmes has told the story of the defeat that was almost as good as a victory in his "Grandmother's Story of Bunker-Hill Battle" (xiii. 149) : —

How, driven, yet scarce defeated, our worn-out men
    retreated,
With their powder-horns all emptied, like the swim-
    mers from a wreck.

A commander-in-chief must be chosen. The army consisted chiefly of northern men, and to unite the colonies it was thought wise to choose a leader from the south. The home of George Washington was in the large and important colony of Virginia. Years before this time, when he was only a young man of twenty-three, he had saved part of Braddock's army at Fort Duquesne, after its leader, too proud to be advised by a colonist, had thrown away the lives of most of his men. It was decided to make Washington commander-in-chief, and he set out for Boston, a ride of eleven days. Lowell describes the army of

which he took command, standing beneath
the old elm at Cambridge ("Under the Old
Elm," xiii. 82). He says: —

> A motley rout was that which came to stare,
> In raiment tanned by years of sun and storm,
> Of every shape that was not uniform,
> Dotted with regimentals here and there;
> An army all of captains, used to pray
> And stiff in fight, but serious drill's despair,
> Skilled to debate their orders, not obey.

This "motley rout" thought their leader cold
and severe, but before long they "learned to
honor first, then love him, then revere."

Washington took for his Cambridge head-
quarters the house which afterwards became
the home of Longfellow. Of this the poet
wrote ("To a Child," i. 230): —

> Once, ah, once, within these walls,
> One whom memory oft recalls,

The Father of his Country, dwelt.
And yonder meadows broad and damp
The fires of the besieging camp
Encircled with a burning belt.
Up and down these echoing stairs,
Heavy with the weight of cares,
Sounded his majestic tread;
Yes, within this very room
Sat he in those hours of gloom,
Weary both in heart and head.

Lowell sums up the course of the war in a few lines of his "Ode for the Fourth of July, 1876" (xiii. 97) : —

Seven years long was the bow
Of battle bent, and the heightening
Storm-heaps convulsed with the throe
Of their uncontainable lightning;
Seven years long heard the sea
Crash of navies and wave-borne thunder;

Then drifted the cloud-rack alee,
And new stars were seen, a world's wonder,
Each by her sisters made bright,
All binding all to their stations,
Cluster of manifold light
Startling the old constellations:
Men looked up and grew pale:
Was it a comet or star,
Omen of blessing or bale,
Hung o'er the ocean afar?

The colonies were free, but, in the midst of their jealousies and their self-seeking, men might well question whether this new union were "comet or star." "Freedom's great experiment," Whittier calls it ("The Vow of Washington," iv. 286), and recalling those troublous days, he voices the thoughts of the countries looking on: —

Could it succeed? Of honor sold
And hopes deceived all history told.

A FRIEND IN THE LIBRARY

Above the wrecks that strewed the mournful past,
Was the long dream of ages true at last?

Thank God! the people's choice was just,
The one man equal to his trust,
Wise beyond lore, and without weakness good,
Calm in the strength of flawless rectitude!

His rule of justice, order, peace,
Made possible the world's release:
Taught prince and serf that power is but a trust,
And rule, alone, which serves the ruled, is just.

So it is that the story of our country is told
by the poets, from the long-ago days of the
northern saga tales to the close of the Revolutionary War, to the times when, although the
land had yet before her many difficulties to
meet and hard questions to solve, she had become the United States of America and had
taken her fate into her own hands.

HISTORY AND BIOGRAPHY

ADDITIONAL

EMERSON

Historical Discourse at Concord, 1635–1835, xi. 27.
Concord Hymn, ix. 158.

LONGFELLOW

Eliot's Oak, iii. 229.
Lady Wentworth, iv. 177.

WHITTIER

The Border War of 1708, vi. 368.
The Black Men in the Revolution and War of 1812, vi. 406.
Norembega, i. 285.
Mabel Martin, i. 195.

LOWELL

Columbus, ix. 154.

HOLMES

King's Chapel, xiii. 311.
Ode for Washington's Birthday, xii. 242.
An Appeal for "The Old South," xiii. 187.

35

A FRIEND IN THE LIBRARY

HAWTHORNE

The Scarlet Letter, vi.
The Gray Champion, i. 1.
The Maypole of Merry Mount, i. 64.
Legends of the Province House, ii. 1.
Endicott and the Red Cross, ii. 276.
Grandfather's Chair, xii. 1.
Mrs. Hutchinson, xvii. 1.
Sir William Phips, xvii. 13.
Sir William Pepperell, xvii. 23.
The Duston Family, xvii. 229.

QUESTIONS

1. Which poem of Longfellow's relates to the earliest voyages to America?

   " The Skeleton in Armor " (i. 63).

2. What other poems has Longfellow written about early American history?

   " Hiawatha " (ii. 121).
   " The Courtship of Miles Standish " (ii. 299).
   " Evangeline " (ii. 17).
   " John Endicott " (v. 335).

"Giles Corey" (v. 445).

"Lady Wentworth" (iv. 177).

" Eliot's Oak" (iii. 229).

3. What was "Master Cheever's" most fa-
   mous work?
   *A Latin textbook, which was used in New
   England for one hundred years.*

4. When was Harvard College founded?
   *In 1636, sixteen years after the first settle-
   ment in Massachusetts.*

5. Who is known as the Apostle to the Indians?
   John Eliot.

6. Why was the difficulty between Puritans
   and Quakers so irreconcilable?
   *Because both were so earnest in their op-
   posing beliefs, and religious liberty was a
   thing of the future.*

7. Which poet has written most of the Quakers in colonial days?

The Quaker Whittier.

8. Why was the matter of witchcraft even more troublesome than the coming of the Quakers?

Because it was the general belief, in Europe as well as in America, not only that such a thing existed, but that it was the direct work of Satan.

9. What poem gives the best idea of witchcraft in New England?

Longfellow's "Giles Corey" (v. 445).

10. What was the subject of Longfellow's first published poem?

A fight with the Indians at Lovell's Pond.

11. What was the most remarkable victory in American history?

The capture of Louisburg.

12. Why may " Evangeline " (ii. 17) be called the masterpiece of Longfellow's longer poems?

    Because of its beauty in form and spirit and its strength.

13. What is the most famous poem about the Revolution?

    Longfellow's " Paul Revere's Ride " (iv. 24).

14. Why are the lines, " And fired the shot heard round the world," and " The fate of a nation was riding that night," so famous?

    Because they say so much in so few words.

15. What three poets wrote of the first day of the Revolution?

    Holmes, Whittier, and Lowell.

16. What is a special charm of Lowell's " Ode Read at the One Hundredth Anniversary of the Fight at Concord Bridge " (xiii. 73)?

    Its sympathy and humanness.

17. What poem describes the battle of Bunker Hill from a woman's point of view?

"Grandmother's Story of Bunker-Hill Battle" by Holmes (xiii. 148).

18. Why was Washington made commander-in-chief?

Because he was a Virginian, and because of his skill in saving the remnant of Braddock's army at Fort Duquesne.

19. Why did Whittier call the Union "Freedom's great experiment"?

Because so many were doubtful of its success.

20. Why was it thought probable that the Union would fail?

Because the different states were so jealous of one another.